The Hour Glass Effect

Leveraging Female Talent
for your
Competitive Advantage

by Dr. Tammy Wong

From the *Fostering Executive Leadership in Women*™ series

ISBN 13: 9781931945851
ISBN 10: 1931945853

Library of Congress Catalog Number: 2008927642

Printed in the United States of America

Printed July 2008

10 09 08 07 6 5 4 3 2 1

 Expert Publishing, Inc.
14314 Thrush Street NW
Andover, MN 55304-3330

Andover,   1-877-755-4966
Minnesota www.expertpublishinginc.com

Table of Contents

Introduction

$\mathscr{I}$n 2003, I had been working in corporate America for almost twenty-five years. I realized I wanted to make more of a difference for organizations and especially the women in them. I chose to go back to school, while still working, and to gain current research and experience in leadership by completing my Ph.D. At one of the companies I worked for, I used my experiences from corporate life, non-profit boards, and the knowledge from my Ph.D. to grow a diverse group of women into one organization that would help them foster their own leadership potential.

Over a period of three years, we grew the organization from three hundred members to over two thousand members worldwide. We organized a board with a vision, mission, executive sponsorship, and clearly defined roles and responsibilities. In 2006, my peers recognized me with the "Making a Difference" award, the highest form of peer recognition in a global company with over thirty-eight thousand employees. We had all come a long way.

Because I strongly believe women's initiatives are an essential, yet missing, part of business success and women are an untapped segment in the workforce, I wrote this book. My purpose is to first show how a company can benefit through an initiative that fosters executive leadership in females and second to demonstrate how such a program can help recruit, retain, and develop them in organizations. This book also provides practical guidelines and attributes for women looking to create or move to a women-friendly company.

Whether you are an executive reading this book to learn more about fostering executive leadership in women or you are a woman who wants to know more about women's initiatives and how you can develop your career by participating in one, consider these three questions as you read this book:

1. How would you describe your company's leadership culture?

2. If your organization has a women's initiative, how has it changed the leadership within your company?

3. If your organization does not have a women's initiative, what can you do to develop one?

I want to continue making a difference for women, sharing with them my experiences and vision of what companies can and should be as women continue to take on executive leadership positions. Leadership is a learned trait. Everyone can learn to lead. The more practice we get through experiences, both personally and professionally, the more we will build our own attributes and values around leadership.

I believe everyone has talent and we need to utilize that talent to the highest degree. I strive to create an environment of trust and compassion and to promote the understanding that every woman has a voice no matter what her experience or job level.

My purpose in writing this book is to help accomplish those goals.

To your success,

Dr. Tammy Wong

Since the early 1990s, corporations have recognized the need to develop executive leadership capability among women managers.

Chapter 1

Don't Ignore the Roar

The world is always changing, but the rate of those changes has accelerated drastically since the middle of the twentieth century. That change is seen in technology, communications, the family, entertainment, and possibly the most significant of all, the workplace. Prior to World War II, the workplace was male-dominated. With few exceptions, males ran the companies.

With the labor shortage that came about during World War II, women filled many positions formerly held by males. This change was considered temporary and necessary, brought on by the unique situations created by the war.

The number of women in the workplace increased dramatically over the next five decades. Women began to demand equal pay for equal work. They rightfully expected equal opportunities based on the results of their work, not their gender. Radios blared with the lyrics from Helen

Reddy's song, "I Am Woman, Hear Me Roar." That roar continues to grow louder.

The 1964 Civil Rights Act made discrimination against women in education or employment illegal. However, the passage of equal opportunity legislation did not ensure equal treatment. Consider the following.

During the five decades from 1950 to 2000, the number of women in the workforce steadily increased. In 2006, women accounted for over 50 percent of the total U.S. labor force, up from 29.6 percent in 1950.[1]

Since 2000, the number of women in executive management positions has grown less than 1 percent annually; women make up less than 15 percent of executives in corporations.[2]

In 2005, only eleven Fortune 500 company CEOs were women. Only half of the 500 companies have more than one female officer. Only four hundred of the Fortune 500 companies have a woman on their board of directors.[3] If this pace continues, the number of women on top corporate boards will not equal the number of men until the year 2064.[4]

At the end of the twentieth century, women reached a critical mass in education. Since 1984, women have outnumbered men in undergraduate and graduate schools. Today women earn a majority of associate's, bachelor's, and master's degrees. They earn 40 percent of doctoral degrees. Women make up 46 percent of those entering law schools and 42 percent of those entering medical schools.

Women are joining the workforce in record numbers. The female labor participation rate of those between the ages of twenty-five and fifty-four is over 75 percent. However, the male participation rate for this age group is a bit over 90 percent.[5] Labor force participation rates among married women increased dramatically from 1966 to 1994, from 35 percent to 61 percent. The increase was even more dramatic for married women with children under three years of age—from

> *The research shows that one woman in ten will get through life with the option to decide whether she wants to work.*

21 percent to 60 percent over the same period. Dual-earner couples are swiftly replacing the traditional married-couple model of breadwinner husband and homemaker wife. From 1970 to 1993, the proportion of dual-earner couples increased from 39 percent to 61 percent of all married couples.[6]

As more businesses adopt flexible work arrangements, offer more child-care options, and pay more, the female labor force disparity will continue to shrink.

The research shows that one woman in ten will get through life with the option to decide whether she wants to work. The other nine will have to work, according to the Board of Labor Statistics.[7] Since women have assumed an increasingly larger segment of the workforce, the need to develop female leadership qualities has become more apparent.

The Need

Since the early 1990s, corporations have recognized the need to develop executive leadership capability among women managers. Three major factors led to this realization.

First, the advent of the quality movement with its dependence on teams necessitated the involvement of women in leadership in the workplace. Today's organizational managers need leadership skills to develop high performing teams and to cover the wider spans of control left in the wake of downsizing, buyouts, and mergers.

Second, the elimination of many middle management positions necessitated women's development as leaders. As we continue to change within our organizations, it is important to hear both female and male perspectives. Many companies are now incorporating this knowledge into their organization's diversity practices. By looking at issues concerning women in the workplace from many different angles, a company will be able to attract and retain highly talented females. Today's organizational managers, both women and men, need leadership skills to develop high performing teams.

Third, organizations in today's business environment are subject to numerous regulatory, economic, competitive, and technological forces that often dictate major organizational change to ensure survival. These turbulent environmental conditions have created a need for executive leadership that effectively guides the organization through these periods of significant change. These changes have forced organizations to adapt quickly and effectively, which puts a premium on executive leadership capable of system-wide organizational change[8]. Women can be significant contributors to solving this problem of organizational change and executive leadership.

Even though women have made significant progress in the corporate structure, they are still short of their potential. There is a shortage of women in significant leadership positions in companies. I believe this shortage comes from a company's lack of understanding on how to develop and retain women in key leadership positions.

The Problem

Many companies suffer from a lack of leadership, yet they do not seem to recognize that leading is a skill that must be purposefully developed. Leadership is a learned skill.

> *It is far healthier and more productive for us to start with the assumption that it is possible for everyone to lead. Leadership is, after all, a set of skills. In addition, skills can be strengthened, honed, and enhanced if we have the proper motivation and desire, along with practice and feedback, role models, and coaching.*[9]

Organizations are recruiting and hiring women, yet they have trouble developing and retaining female executives and advancing them into ranks of senior management.[10]

Despite inroads in some executive ranks, the progress of women into top-level management positions has been slow.

Corporate culture is a fundamental reason for women's absence from management and executive leadership positions. For a culture to advance women, it has to have a formal succession plan and leadership development program that addresses not only the employees at the vice president and director levels, but also one to two levels below. It has to track the number of women within its leadership ranks and what has been formally implemented to advance these women.

Mentoring is the key deliverable in this area, as is accountability for development plans and documented paths for employees' success and promotion within the company.

My own success came when I worked in companies that had clear development plans that both the employee and manager developed and tracked together. Employees were not left to track their development plans on their own. Both the employee and manager were accountable for the employee's success. Together, they worked on overcoming the barriers for growth.

Catalyst, a research and advocacy group for working women, conducted a study of women at the vice president level and above in Fortune 1000 companies in the United States. The study compared the experience and perception of women in 2003 with those in the same positions in 1996. Catalyst

Despite inroads in some executive ranks, the progress of women into top-level management positions has been slow.

found that many businesses had not yet adopted policies to promote women to executive leadership positions and the barriers had not changed in eight years.

The women in the Catalyst study cited nine corporate barriers that affected women's future growth:

1. Limited management or line experience for women.

2. Lack of mentoring and role models for women at the highest levels.

3. Exclusion of women from informal networks and channels of communication where important information on organizational politics and decision-making is shared.

4. Established stereotypes and preconceptions of women's roles, abilities, commitment, and leadership style.

5. Restrictive or inflexible work schedules.

6. Absence of career and succession planning.

7. Counterproductive behavior of male co-workers, including taking credit for women's contributions.

8. Lenience toward sexual harassment.

9. Attributing women's success to tokenism.[11]

The study by Catalyst also found a link between a higher number of women in a company's executive ranks and its bottom-line performance. The group of companies with the highest representation of women on their top management teams experienced better financial performance than the group of companies with the lowest women's representation.

Companies with the highest percentage of women in top leadership positions had a 35.1 percent higher return on equity and reported a 34 percent higher total return to shareholders.[12]

Without a purposeful approach to addressing these issues, companies will continue to have difficulty attracting and retaining talent from a large segment of the workforce —females. Corporate leaders that fail to take the initiative to develop and foster leadership in women will find themselves scrambling for talent to make their corporations survive and thrive in this demanding and changing business environment.

Demographics play an important role in the current and future hiring decisions of most companies. For the first time in U.S history, we have four generations in the workplace: Traditionalists born from 1922–1945, Baby Boomers born from 1946–1964, Gen X born from 1965–1984, and Gen Y born from 1985–2003. Baby Boomers, Gen Y, and Gen X have populations of 78 million, 48 million, and 80 million, respectively. Visually this demographic is in the shape of an hourglass and the hourglass could also depict the shape of a woman. Companies will continue looking for skilled and talented employees to meet their needs now and in the future.

The answer will be women—The Hour Glass Effect.

The Solution

I've long believed that a women's initiative is the key to fostering female leadership within an organization. The results of the Catalyst study supported my belief and encouraged me to continue my research in the area of women's initiatives.

What I found is that a women's initiative can take on many different forms. It can be as simple as an internal women's networking organization that meets periodically to discuss women's work issues, hear a speaker on a women's leadership topic, or provide training that is particularly useful to female leaders.

A women's initiative can take on a much broader scope that includes a life cycle, which includes a formal process to develop the concept, the launch, and the execution of the initiative. The approach I developed is broken into five different steps. These steps include the following.

1. **Concept:** Developing a new women's initiative or the improvement of the current initiative.

2. **Plan:** Building the framework for the initiative, determining what is needed, creating a task force, and determining the success factors for the program.

3. **Integrate:** Deciding who will benefit from the initiative, who will be part of the initiative, determining who will lead the initiative, analyzing what marketing impact there will be both internally and externally to the company.

4. **Launch:** Announcing the initiative to the organization.

5. **Execute:** Tracking the success of the initiative, timelines, and activities associated with the women's initiative.

In my research, I talked with leaders in companies with women's initiatives and found the leaders to be both supportive and even somewhat surprised at the positive results from their women's initiative.

One leader said:

> *Everyone just assumed women were leaving to stay home to start having a family and raising their children, when, in fact, the results of the task force revealed something quite different. They discovered women were not leaving the firm to stay home; they were leaving the firm to go to our competitors, or they were leaving the firm to start their own businesses.*

Another leader noted:

> *The important thing is the board realizes the women's initiative is important. They realize we can't grow our business without women, and they realized everything we do seems to affect our entire culture, and have made it [the women's initiative] so; our CEO is in support of it.*

Women play a vital role in leadership that often goes untapped. Successful companies recognize this potential and address the issue through positive action. One such action is having a women's initiative that can be expected to influence organizational growth, development, inclusion, flexibility, and foster executive leadership in women.

Women play a vital role in leadership that often goes untapped.

The world is indeed changing and so is the workplace. Companies that thrive are willing to change. If change leads to improvements, the sooner change is implemented, the quicker the improvements will come.

The roar is not going away. The population of women and their potential in the workplace is too big to ignore. Don't ignore the roar.

～

Things to Consider

- ❑ How many women are in leadership positions in our company?

- ❑ What changes have occurred in the last ten years in our company regarding the ratio of male/females in leadership?

- ❑ How does the turnover ratio of women compare to the turnover ratio of men in our company?

- ❑ How do our company's training and retention programs address the specific needs of female employees?

- ❑ How would our employees rate our company as effective in developing and retaining female leaders?

- ❑ How would those outside our company rate our company as effective in developing and retaining female leaders?

A purposeful women's initiative can have significant positive results for a company.

*D*emographics play an important role in the current and future hiring decisions of most companies.

Chapter 2

What to Expect

$\mathscr{A}$ women's initiative can have dramatic results in recruiting, training, and lowering turnover or retention costs for a company and its women. The decision to begin a women's initiative must be based on the potential results.

I've found the primary result of a women's initiative is to create a woman-friendly organization, one that can attract and retain talented women who can make a significant contribution to the company both in the growth and financial results of the company, thus affecting the bottom line.

Women with skills, talent, and education who are pursuing careers have many options today. Working in a woman-friendly company is often a criterion. I've identified five ways a woman can determine if a company is woman-friendly.

How to Recognize a Woman-Friendly Company

1. The company has been listed for ten or more years on *Working Mother* magazine's list of 100 Best Companies for Working Women.

2. A component of managers' pay is associated with the advancement of women in the corporation. This can be found in both the *Working Mother* magazine's list and also through contact with the company or, in some instances, the company will post this information on its web site.

3. The company has won the Catalyst Award symbolizing achievement in the advancement of women. The company applies for this nomination through Catalyst. Catalyst goes through a very formal process of verifying the information and facts and awards the few selected companies, the Catalyst Award. (This award has been bestowed since 1987 to companies that develop and advance women in business.)[1]

4. A women's initiative is promoted on the company's web site and contact information is available.

5. The company has a staff position dedicated to the advancement of women.

With this knowledge, an individual can identify those companies that are women friendly and companies can use these five criteria to create an environment where women with high-potential, desirable talents and skills, and valuable experience will want to work.

Sometimes Surprising Results

All successful initiatives that I've studied have one thing in common: the CEO has communicated the vision and direction to the organization to create a paradigm shift in the culture. In addition, a team of people has to take ownership of the initiative, to do the heavy lifting within the initiative life cycle from concept to execution.

In my interviews with leaders from companies with women's initiatives, many described how the initiatives changed and transformed the culture. They expressed a deep cultural support of the women's initiative. Many of the leaders had been at the company before the creation of the initiative. With pride, they shared much of the change that had taken place within the company over the last few years.

How a Women's Initiative Impacts a Company

A purposeful women's initiative can impact both the women and the company through specific areas. Here are just a few that I've identified through my own experience and research. A women's initiative can:

1. Provide the mechanism to develop women's leadership skills within the organization. The women's initiative provides these leadership roles and development within the initiative.

2. Increase the understanding of the role of gender in the organization through documented research, practice, and the current climate of the company.

3. Transform the organization's culture significantly into one that is inclusive of women at all levels of the hierarchy.

4. Promote essential mentoring opportunities for women, both formally and informally, within the organization

through peer, team, and executive mentoring. This has the greatest impact for female leadership development.

In the following chapters you will read about each of these topics. You'll find relevant information that will give you insight as well as practical ideas you can put to work.

~

Things to Consider

❑ Has our company thought of creating a women's initiative?

❑ How many people in our company support a women's initiative? Does our CEO support the initiative?

❑ How would our company fund a women's initiative?

❑ If we currently have a women's initiative, how do we communicate and share information?

❑ If we have multiple locations, how do best practices and new ideas get communicated to the entire company to create support for our women's initiative?

A woman has the
qualities to be a leader,
but if a company does not provide
the opportunity to lead,
that leadership ability could
remain dormant.

Chapter 3

Developing Women as Leaders

Leadership is the key to successfully building and sustaining any organization. Successful companies place a high value on developing leadership in women and do so through a women's initiative. After all, leaders are developed, not born.

Learning to lead occurs from trial and error, observation of others, networking, and both formal and continuing education. Any company that wants to have a strong leadership base with loyalty to the company must focus on developing that leadership from within. When a company builds leadership from within its own ranks, employee satisfaction increases. Satisfied employees remain with the corporation for longer periods of time, and the company avoids the high cost of employee turnover. Likewise, a company that overcomes obstacles to developing executive leadership in women will be able to retain quality women employees at all levels.

A woman has the qualities to be a leader, but if a company does not provide the opportunity to lead, that leadership ability could remain dormant. Two things cause this. First, low turnover among current leaders. And, second, artificial barriers, such as "hidden" biases against females, older employees, minorities, etc. Each of these situations prevents people with leadership qualities from having the opportunity to express and develop those traits. Often such biases take on the form of both positive and negative labels, such as high potential or non-performer.

Throughout my career, I've noticed that many companies employ a practice of labeling employees. It's usually an informal practice; labels aren't written down, but are spoken of as part of the culture. Different labels are used, even with positive intentions. For example, star, fast-tracker, and high-potential, are all labels assigned to people who exhibit highly valuable traits and the potential to develop into an executive or leader. Usually these labels are assigned early in a woman's career. But what happens to such a person after five years and five managers? Companies have to continue to motivate and develop people through talent development objectives and programs and continually track an employee's growth potential.

Many employees have reported to me throughout my career. I have found that, rather than assigning impersonal labels, discovering what an employee is good at and what she has a passion for works towards both identifying and developing her strengths.

A few years ago, when a female employee joined my organization, several of her previous managers had passed her up for promotions. In seeking to understand why this happened, I found it was much more of a personal issue with members of the leadership team than any lack of skill and experience on the part of the employee. After a review of the previous three years of this employee's career, it became evident that her leadership was not only excellent, but exceptional. She just needed more opportunities for visibility and communication to the current leadership team to demonstrate the leadership traits that had been documented and developed.

Any company that wants to expand female leadership will seek to provide the opportunities for employees of both genders.

Successful leadership is often equated with progression within a corporation, yet involves both professional and personal advancement. Professional advancement includes pay, position, and promotions. Personal advancement includes:

- personal investment in education and work experience;
- individual characteristics such as personality traits and psychological factors that affect the ability to manage and lead others;
- interpersonal systems, including supportive relationships and peer networks; and
- personal factors, including a family, marital status, significant other, dependents, aging parents, and friends.

Given all these considerations, it's easy to see that women need to use several strategies to be effective leaders. These include:

- finding a mentor and creating alliances,
- networking with other leaders,
- knowing how to create visibility for themselves,
- communicating effectively,
- taking risks,
- integrating work and home, and
- understanding gender traits of women and men.

One of the most powerful things a woman can do to further her leadership potential is to understand that many different approaches to leadership exist. My research and experience show that women are generally not well-suited to all leadership styles, particularly authoritarian or autocratic approaches. Women tend to be more comfortable with, and accepted when they use, the servant leadership, emotional intelligence, or charismatic styles.

Servant Leadership Style

An emerging approach to leadership and service is termed "servant leadership." This style of leadership puts serving others as the number one priority.[1] The model looks like an inverted pyramid poised on its sharp point. The leader, now on the bottom, serves and supports high-level managers who, in turn, serve and support middle managers who serve and support the personnel who report to them.

Servant leadership assumes the role of the leader is to serve the organization and individuals within it. The servant leader approach is both serving and leading. Servant leaders are focused on making a difference to create positive change. Relationships take precedence or priority over the

> *Servant leaders are focused on making a difference to create positive change.*

task and product. In addition, the servant leader is primarily motivated by a desire to serve and to see life as a mission, not a career.

Servant leadership encourages everyone to balance leading and serving within his or her own life. It reminds people who are in leadership positions that one's primary responsibility is to serve others. It encourages people who are in follower positions to look for situational opportunities to provide leadership.

The first example that comes to mind for this type of leadership is Mother Teresa. She was born in 1910 and dedicated her life to not only helping others, but also in leading them. In 1948, she was granted permission to start a school in the slums of Calcutta to teach the children of the poor. In 1950, she formed a group of women who became known as the Missionaries of Charity. This organization grew from twelve members to thousands serving the poorest of the poor in 450 centers around the world. She was one of the pioneers of established homes for AIDS victims. She gained worldwide acclaim for her tireless efforts on behalf of world peace and received the Nobel Prize in 1979. In receiving the award, she asked that the banquet funds be sent to the poor in Calcutta. This money would feed hundreds of poor people. Because of Mother Teresa's servant leadership, the Missionaries of Charity is still in existence today with thousands still serving the poor around the world.

I believe as leaders that we are there to not only achieve the goals and objectives of the business, but also to do everything possible to develop employees into leaders and to help all employees see their true potential in current and future positions. This is one way we can exhibit servant leadership. Another form of leadership that women seem to be comfortable with is emotional intelligence.

Emotional Intelligence Leadership Style

The emotional intelligence leadership style encompasses social, emotional, and intellectual aspects. It includes self-control, zeal, persistence, and the ability to motivate oneself.[2]

Four central domains are used to describe emotional intelligence: self-awareness, self-management, social awareness, and relationship management. Emotional intelligence is the capacity to handle one's emotions and relationships. Leaders who have emotional intelligence have the ability to perceive and express emotions, to understand and use them, and to manage them to foster personal growth.[3] It is not surprising those individuals who are able to assess their own and others' emotions and appropriately adapt their behavior to a given situation based on this assessment are expected to be leaders.[4]

Successful leaders use emotional intelligence when they deliver helpful critiques, value diversity, and network effectively. Emotional competency is not a handicap but a criterion for successful performance. It is a style that is effective for both women and men and important to both middle managers and executives.

Effective leaders use emotional intelligence to inspire employees and instill an enthusiasm to perform beyond their job descriptions.

I found this to be particularly true during my three years as the president of a women's organization where I worked. The board included many women in various positions of leadership within the company. It was clear from the beginning that each and every woman, no matter what her position, had something to add based on her experience. By valuing each woman's contributions, we were able to capitalize on many strengths and built an organization based on trust. The organization thrived as a result.

Effective leaders use emotional intelligence to inspire employees and instill an enthusiasm to perform beyond their job descriptions.

Ann Mulcahy, CEO of Xerox Corporation, is an excellent example of a woman who uses the emotional intelligence leadership style. In 1998, I was Mulcahy's facilitator for a Xerox Corporation women's conference. As each person came into the room, Mulcahy walked up to her, shook hands, and introduced herself. I was impressed with her leadership style. When Mulcahy took over as CEO in 2001, the company was on the verge of Chapter 11 bankruptcy. The company had over $17 billion in debt and had recorded losses in each of the preceding six years. Customers were unhappy and the economy for technology was slowing.

Mulcahy brought the best out of her team. She spent the first ninety days on planes traveling to various offices and listening to anyone who had a perspective on what was wrong with the company and what steps needed to be taken to improve performance and customer satisfaction.

Mulcahy believes that when an organization is struggling, employees need to know what's happening and that the leadership has a strategy to fix it. Beyond that, leaders have to tell people what they can do to help. In return, Mulcahy gained total support from her executive team and employees. She created a dedicated workforce aligned around a common set of objectives. In 2007, Mulcahy held the number five position on Forbes 100 Most Influential Women list.

I believe emotional intelligence sets leaders apart from others—their organizations go far, they influence people, and retain positive productive relationships. They are able to align objectives among teams. Women who use emotional intelligence are usually strong leaders. Another leadership style women prefer is the charismatic style.

Charismatic Leadership Style

The charismatic leadership model relies on charisma as the mechanism through which leaders influence organizational culture and other significant changes in the workplace.[5] Charismatic leaders have the ability to allure followers and captivate their attention; they give the perception of being effective in bringing about change. They have a vision or mission that transfers to the group. Those who follow charismatic leaders have

> *Charismatic leaders have the ability to allure followers and captivate their attention; they give the perception of being effective in bringing about change.*

more commitment, motivation, and job satisfaction.[6]

The challenge of the charismatic leader is to have substance in addition to style. The impact of leadership must transfer from being mystical to being practical. Servant and emotional leadership styles tend to work well in an organizational structure that resembles an upside down pyramid, whereas charismatic leaders may tend to work in a more traditional hierarchical environment. All three leadership styles involve developing relationships within the organization and improving overall culture.

Most of my experience has been with hierarchical companies. Most recently, I worked with a company that uses a matrix form of management—where an individual may have multiple sources of direction across the organization. The companies with the most promising cultures had leaders who developed relationships in different divisions, business units, and outside companies. I spoke with a long time business associate about a company that we had both worked with and agreed it was a great organization. After further discussion, we concluded it that what made it great were the people. The people with whom we had made connections, friendships, and business decisions, made the difference.

Oprah Winfrey is a great example of a charismatic leader. She began her nationally syndicated show in 1986, and it has remained the number one talk show, largely due to the approach she uses to deliver her message to the audience. Her show is seen by an estimated 48 million viewers a week in the United States and is broadcasted internationally in 126 countries. She brings authenticity and natural experience to all her endeavors. One endeavor in particular is expanding her interest in growing leadership in girls by establishing schools in underdeveloped nations. Oprah encourages viewers to make a difference in the lives of others, which led to the creation of the public charity, Oprah's Angel Network. She has been voted as one of the one hundred most influential people in the world.

Oprah demonstrates charisma. I believe a charismatic leader will attract followers sooner than one who uses the other leadership styles previously outlined. When a woman's first style is charismatic, she has to be able to attract both women and men followers to build relationships, and then use either emotional intelligence or servant leadership styles to sustain the leader-follower relationship.

How a Women's Initiative Can Help a Company Develop Leadership in Women

Those who are involved in a women's initiative develop their leadership skills in a number of ways. First, they may be involved in the leadership within the initiative organization itself. Second, they potentially have more access to executives through events sponsored by the women's initiative, and third, they are more likely to find mentors than if they were not involved in the initiative.

I worked with one company that had a women's initiative in place for over a decade. The question of why the company participated in the women's initiative became a key point of conversation with the executive national director. When asked why the company would commit the time, energy, and money required to continue the women's initiative, her immediate reaction was this:

When people think of the women's initiative, they think a lot about what we do to develop them into leaders. This includes developmental awareness to the company about gender issues in regards to inclusion of women and men in the entire company. The company's past and present CEOs have been supportive of this initiative. Because they have seen the results, the women's initiative has impacted the entire firm.

She went on to emphasize that retention of women is a core value and a priority for the corporation. The executives at the very top of the organization and the board of directors are conscious of the pool of talent in the organization. Other leaders responded similarly when asked about why they were personally involved with the women's initiative.

One leader said:

The biggest kind of a-ha to me about our women's initiative was that it relates to retaining and supporting our best women so that they become our best leaders.

Another said:

It also forces leaders around the country to identify, develop, and bring forth talented women executives.

Yet another leader stated:

The leaders within the women's initiative have been forced to stretch beyond their comfort zones and allowed to learn about other parts of the firm that they wouldn't otherwise be exposed to.

A key finding from my research was the impact the women's initiative can have on existing leaders. One leader stated:

The initiative has definitely personally affected me, and I think about it in everything that I do—we need to make things easier on our women so that we can keep them here, and, in turn, save the firm money in turnover costs, recruiting, training, etc.

An initiative has the ability to affect the culture, communication, and the way a leader leads. The initiative affects all these areas and shows the impact an initiative can have on a company.

～

Things to Consider

❑ How does our company leadership exhibit the servant leadership style?

❑ How does our company leadership exhibit the emotional intelligence leadership style?

❑ How does our company leadership exhibit the charismatic leadership style?

❑ Which style is dominant in our company and why do we select that style?

❑ Which style best describes my personal leadership practices and why do I select that style?

❑ How would those outside our company describe the leadership style of our company?

A women's initiative,
properly set in motion,
creates positions on the
leadership staff that include
both women and men leaders.

Chapter 4

The Role of Gender In the Organization

The study of gender roles in corporations is a fascinating one for me. It includes not only what goes on in the workplace, but also what goes on in society at large, particularly in the family.

I had always wanted four boys since I had grown up in a family of three girls. After our fourth son was born, my husband and I decided to have a fifth child. My husband had come from a family of five. I had an ultrasound late in my eighth month of this pregnancy, and my doctor asked me if I wanted to know the sex of the child. I said, "Sure." The doctor said, "It's a girl." What a shock! After four boys, you really do believe the next one will be a boy. It took several months after my daughter's birth for me to believe I had a girl, but also to see she was very different from her brothers. Her sleep cycle, her way of being aware of so many things around her, her cry, and her need to be held were all different. It was fascinating.

Gender differences are the most basic and pervasive of all differences. Children begin to assume their roles very early in life.

As children, boys compete as a means of ordering themselves in a hierarchy of talents, strengths, and abilities. As adults, they tend to order themselves in hierarchical ways within organizations. Males tend to think in a linear, sequential, concrete, and logical mode, making decisions by lining up data consecutively and objectively to get a bottom-line answer. Female programming is much different.

As children, girls are typically verbal and relational. Females often switch between the linear left and intuitive right sides of their brains. They tend to be subjective and reflective. Women's major aim in listening is to communicate interest and caring; men's major aim is to get information.

I try to make an effort to spend quality time with each of my children individually on a weekly basis. I have discovered one of the best ways to do this is while driving them to an event or by walking or bike riding together. This is a very effective way to learn about each of them.

What is fascinating is the difference in communication. The boys are succinct, to the point, and they usually share what has happened recently regarding sports and school. My daughter, on the other hand, speaks about people, the future, where she thinks she is going to be in a few years, how many children she would like to have, etc. Once she taught me a song I had never heard before.

I cannot remember a time that any of my sons ever wanted to teach me a song that we could both sing together. My sons and daughter have different interests. What motivates my sons may or may not provide the same motivation to my daughter. They are different. Likewise, women and men may have different motivations in their professional lives.

Family imprinting significantly affects girls and family life has a profound impact on their self-esteem. Parents often expect their daughters to be academically proficient and behave in demure, feminine ways. Girls are usually taught to be quiet, somewhat dependent, polite, and well mannered. Those traits may increase harmony in girl-boy relationships, but they do not necessarily guarantee success in females' professional careers. Spirited and aggressive at ages eight and nine, girls begin to lose more confidence than boys do in their abilities at ages thirteen and fourteen.

Girls are taught to follow the rules, whereas boys are often encouraged to challenge those same rules

Girls are taught to follow the rules, whereas boys are often encouraged to challenge those same rules and act independently.

and act independently. Girls learn to be quiet and obedient because they were punished for not doing so; they earned praise from parents, teachers, and almost everyone else when they acted liked good girls. Boys tend to be able to have more leeway in acting independently and take more risks.

One time our four boys were jumping off a plastic playhouse into the grass. Our daughter, being the youngest, wanted to do the same thing. As she got on the roof, my husband said, "No, she's going to get hurt." I told her, "Go for it!" She jumped off the roof, rolled into the grass, and leaped to her feet. She had a huge smile on her face. She had jumped off the playhouse just like her older brothers. She had taken a risk and succeeded.

In adulthood, following the rules can be detrimental to a woman's career.

The real tragedy is that, despite the pats on the shoulder and the compliments, being a good girl actually undermines your career and prevents you from achieving maximum success. The rewards go to women who make their own rules, take big chances, toot their own horns, and don't worry if everyone likes them.[1]

I have found being involved in my children's schools has been beneficial to me. Seeing the differences within the education system is very interesting. Our educational system has changed over the last few years. Previously, there was a tremendous difference in the classroom. Teachers would allow boys to shout out answers, but girls were asked to raise their hands. This has changed in the upper grades, fourth and above, and the teachers are usually consistent in having everyone raise their hands. I also notice I receive many more calls from the teachers about my sons for acting up in class, than I receive on my daughter. The negative attention my sons receive seems to be rewarded by additional attention when I meet with the teachers and my sons. My daughter, on the other hand, has learned the rules of being quiet.

Is this always good? I am not sure. I am interested in how we can create an atmosphere for both girls and boys to understand and work with their differences in the classroom. I believe gender training at a young age will help. It will also benefit the teachers if they have a better understanding of the traits of their students. As children involved in such training grow older, the results will also be transferred to the workplace.

Typical characteristics of gender roles have been identified in research, but are by no means universal or exclusive. These roles tend to be embedded in individuals from a very young age and are not alleviated during adulthood.

As girls develop into women, their natural skills and interests tend to show marked divergence from the roles that are typically fostered in males. As adults, women are naturally more interested in socialization than hierarchical position. A survey conducted by Deloitte and Touche found that women are more likely to associate female success with skill, accessibility to female mentors, and education. Men, on the other hand, are more likely to attribute women's success to the prosperous economy of the last ten years.[2]

Understanding the Male Influence at Work

Male preferences dominate the organizational landscape. It seems that organizations define the ideal worker as someone who prioritizes work above all other needs in life and never takes time off for raising children. Even a casual glance reveals that both formal and traditional career advancement systems have been based on the ideal of the married male manager.

When it comes to career and fatherhood, high-achieving men do not have to deal with difficult trade-offs. A study showed that 30 percent of the women interrupted their careers for child rearing, while virtually none of the men did so. Three-fourths of the male leaders who reported wanting children had them and had significantly more children than did the women leaders. The research shows that the more successful the man, the more likely he will find a spouse and become a father. The opposite holds true for a woman.[3]

Understanding Women in the Context of Work

Women tend to impose cultural norms on themselves that sometimes hold them back at work. Women who prepare for demanding professions are affected much more than men regarding marriage, time of marriage, and when or if to have children. Women still have difficulty negotiating successfully for full partnerships at home, which may influence the work environments they select, thus requiring them to find many ways to cope with the inequities that exist.

Women are far more involved in raising children than men are. The fact that women bear children sets the stage for the role of women as primary caregivers and the expectation that their career development will be sacrificed in order to fulfill this role.

The moment a child is born, many couples assume traditional gender roles despite other intentions.[4] The current generation of women feel like more inferior mothers than those of the previous generation, while men, even with minimal participation at home, feel like better fathers.

With the ability to keep so many balls in the air—juggling priorities and leading a multidimensional life in which she holds a job, raises a family, and runs a household, along with being a spouse—women feel stretched to achieve more.

Many view the need to deal with multiple and often competing work and family priorities as a woman's issue rather than a societal concern. In addition, women often impose this viewpoint on themselves.

When they become mothers, professional women often feel they have to prove themselves again and again. Under the scrutiny of fellow workers and employers, many feel the need to hide their human side when taking time out of their business day to attend a school event, handle a child care issue, or make time for a child's doctor appointment. Women often learn to not discuss family issues, especially children, at work, unless they are speaking to a friend.

Some women prefer to retain full responsibility for home and children because of the power of gender role stereotype. Similarly, men are not strongly supported in American culture for any role but that of breadwinner; both women and men find this gender role message particularly powerful.

The Woman's Juggling Act

Women continue to pay a high personal price for their involvement in careers and for taking primary responsibility for home and family. Whenever women talk about balance in their lives, they generally focus on the need for more time in the day to fulfill their many roles.

I do not believe in balance. If you have ever experienced being on a teeter-totter or see-saw with someone bigger or smaller than yourself, you know balance is very hard to achieve. Shouldn't we be asking our leaders how we integrate both our professional and personal lives? The X & Y generations are asking this question and will work for employers that help them integrate their lives.

I believe I am happiest and the best at both work and home when I have been able to integrate both well. I have always worked and my longest paid time off was my eight-week maternity leave. I believe you have to integrate yourself personally and professionally. I never use the word balance to describe a goal for my life. As a female playing the varied roles of executive, wife, mother, board member, etc., you need to be able to prioritize different events in your life and do those roles well when necessary. I have not been able to attend every school event that included or honored each of my children. However, when I was able to attend one of their events, they knew I had taken the time to spend it with them.

As a mother who works outside the home, I use an easy technique to help me make decisions about which events to attend. I discuss with my children which events they would like me to attend. They can each pick one or two events a month, and they know that I will schedule everything else around these decisions. I put these events on my calendar just as I do business meetings or other commitments. I encourage you to make your personal time an extension of your professional time. This is just one way to learn how to manage your various roles.

Traditional gender roles distract both women and men from achieving true balance in their lives. The real challenge is to balance the feminine and masculine sides of women's natures rather than trying to juggle the demands imposed by society. This challenge becomes even more pronounced as male gender preferences are considered.

The most frequently mentioned female concerns are workload and work/home conflicts. These concerns are elicited particularly in a culture in which high effort, achievement, and competition are the rule. These cultural values require an almost total surrender to the job, which more women than men experience as difficult to achieve. Many women perceive work/home conflicts as an important barrier for accepting a top management position.

Setting the tone for gender equity does not require the exclusion of talented men, but it does require the criteria for leadership to be broadened to include talented women. Leadership should not exclude those women and men who are family-oriented, and who have goals and priorities that exclude working extremely long days, seldom taking vacation or a day off. The desire for personal or family time and the passion to be highly successful in business are not mutually exclusive. There is a place for work and a place for home in the life of a successful leader. To share this example with your family that work and life can co-exist helps set up a new generation of workplace leaders.

When the gender nature of organizations is ignored, companies experience a high level of turnover among women managers and executives. This turnover costs companies in several ways. They lose the substantial investment they have made in a manager's development. Turnover compromises corporations' efforts to increase organizational diversity and it hurts their overall effectiveness.

Some companies are losing talented women with strong records who are working between the levels of manager and director. The assumption that women leave companies to stay home to start having families and raise their children may not be valid. They

> *When the gender nature of organizations is ignored, companies experience a high level of turnover among women managers and executives.*

may be leaving to go to competitors that provide greater opportunities for women, or they may be leaving to start their own business.

In some companies, the transition to fostering an environment that is women-friendly requires only minor adjustments. Others may require a radical cultural change.

How a Women's Initiative Can Help a Company Understand Gender and Its Influence on the Workplace

For one company, the event that triggered the creation of a women's initiative occurred in early 1992, when the CEO found only four out of fifty candidates for senior positions were women, even though the firm had been hiring men and women in equal numbers since 1980.[6] He also noticed a large number of women were leaving the company and not staying long enough to make it to a senior position. Women made up half the labor pool. The CEO stated:

If the firm couldn't stop the flight of the female talent, its ability to serve clients successfully and meet growth targets would be threatened.

The CEO put together a task force to do a year-long study and understand the problem of retention. The task force worked with various outside experts in both researching and gathering data. The task force also met with major corporations who are recognized as leaders in retaining and advancing women to identify best practices and determine why women were leaving the company.

The task force learned three amazing things.

1. Many women viewed the culture of the company to be male dominated.

2. Women perceived they had limited opportunities for advancement.

3. Both women and men needed help in coping with the demands of their professional and personal lives.

The company's leadership had assumed that the women were leaving to raise families. In reality, the majority left to work elsewhere.

One leader stated:

When people think of the women's initiative, they think a lot about what we do to develop women into leaders in terms of bringing awareness to the company about gender issues.

Another leader said:

How men communicate and how women communicate, it's quite different. And understanding . . . the reasons for that and making sure that our women communicate in the same way, or are understood in the same way men are, is important to our company.

A women's initiative, properly set in motion, creates positions on the leadership staff that include both women and men leaders. In most situations, bringing a man onto the leadership team actually encourages men to be interested in and perhaps even get involved in the women's initiative. Men on the leadership team provide different points of view.

Men also can express how the process is progressing, and they can educate other men on more familiar topics that are of interest to men. In addition, many of the programs that are created to solve different issues for women will ultimately positively affect men, too. When a company takes actions designed to improve the production of employees, both women and men will benefit. They learn from each other and everyone gains. For example, both women and men can encourage flexibility and diversity. Men might not openly say, "We would like more flexibility," but giving everybody more flexibility could benefit women as well as men.

The challenge for leaders is to understand gender role differences and understand how to utilize their strengths within their companies. Doing so will impact the entire organization and the company's ability to utilize women and men as the valuable resources they are.

~

Things to Consider

❑ What evidence of accepting gender roles do I see in our company?

❑ How are positions filled in our company and are they filled with a high proportion of women, men, or both?

❑ In what ways do our company's policies add to the work/home conflict? How do our policies affect one gender more than the other, or is the effect the same on both females and males?

Each company has
its own culture
and the culture includes
how women are viewed
in the context of the
organizational hierarchy.

Chapter 5

Women and Organizational Culture

*A*n organization's culture can be described in three layers.[1]

1. The first and innermost layer is made up of the values and beliefs of the leaders in the company. This layer is not as obvious as the other two layers.

2. The second layer includes the policies and procedures of the organization, which are typically derived from the values and beliefs of leaders.

3. The third, and most visible layer, is comprised of the behaviors and actions of leaders and employees. What a company's top leaders believe and value is most evident in the policies and procedures they support and how those policies and procedures are applied.

When it comes to women in the workplace, the beliefs and values of the top executives are evident in policies and procedures that support and advance women. The beliefs and values of executives, usually males, are often established long before they become top leaders.

Organizational culture has a significant impact on how women are viewed and how they view themselves at work. Virtually every society's culture differentiates between female and male behavior in terms of what is appropriate and acceptable. When a specific behavior pattern or role is associated with one gender, the other gender often drops it.

> *Organizational culture has a significant impact on how women are viewed and how they view themselves at work.*

Each company has its own culture, and the culture includes how women are viewed in the context of the organizational hierarchy. Some companies are more purposeful than others when it comes to gender equity. Setting the tone for gender equity does not require the exclusion of talented men, but it does require the criteria for leadership be broadened to include women.

The Effect of Corporate Values and Beliefs on Women

Corporations tend to have ideals that are based on male preferences because of the long tradition of male dominance in the workplace. These norms can be deeply entrenched and difficult to change.

Organizational ideals may include:

- having a structure that supports a focus on work before family,

- paying higher wages to men than women, even for similar work,
- requiring leaders to be willing to dedicate long hours to work.

These organizational norms are a reflection of the values and beliefs of the leaders in the organization, both past and present.

Sometimes deep-seated values and beliefs go unchallenged and perpetuate problems within the organization. A company may have a culture that prevents women from moving into key positions.

Despite attempts to exclude them from key jobs, women still try to gain entry. As women break into more male-dominated occupations, men tend to impose more barriers to entry. Often women are held to higher promotion standards than men with comparable achievements. For a woman, perceptions about how well she has adapted to a male-defined culture play a major role in her becoming a real player in the organization. Because there are a small number of senior executive women, only a limited number of studies examine the differences between female and male leaders. One such study conducted by the Center of Creative Leadership in North Carolina concluded:

> *In order to approach the highest levels, women are*
> *expected to have more strengths and fewer faults than*

> *For a woman, perceptions about how well she has adapted to a male-defined culture play a major role in her becoming a "real player" in the organization.*

their male counterparts. Developing a style with which male managers are comfortable is critical to their career success and is an indication that senior women are still required to fit into a male dominated culture.[2]

The basic issue is that high-achieving women know they must make significant compromises in order to survive in organizations in which careers are patterned after the stereotypical male experience. Research confirms that perception. For example, one analysis shows that female business leaders are furthest from the conventional family ideal for women. These women leaders had a high rate of childlessness, low marriage rate, relatively high divorce rate, and low child care and housework performance. They gained in their profession, but sacrificed in their family relations.[3]

As a result of ignoring the gender aspects of organizational culture, many companies are experiencing a high level of turnover among women managers and executives. This failure costs companies in several ways—they lose the substantial investment they have made in a manager's development, they compromise their efforts to increase organizational diversity, and they hurt their overall effectiveness. Overall, they put the company at a competitive disadvantage.

How Sub-Cultures Influence the Advancement of Women

Organizations rarely have a single, homogenous culture, particularly if they are large and highly matrixed. The company may have an overall set of beliefs and values that its leaders attempt to promote as the company's primary culture, yet there may be subcultures within the organization that operate from other perspectives. One of those perspectives is based on gender. And, surprisingly, the subcultures around gender are not as clear-cut as one would think.

Two studies looked at women's motives to pursue a career in top management. The common conclusion was that men adhere to organizational norms more than women do.[4,5]

This culture consists of traits that are typically considered masculine, including stereotypical masculine styles of communication, approaches to conflict, images of leadership organization, and definitions of success and good management.

Masculinity in an organization is characterized in several ways. The promotion of independence, autonomy, hierarchical relations, competition, task orientation, the establishment of status and authority—all are masculine characteristics. Femininity, conversely, is described as the promotion of a relational self, maintaining balance in life activities, participation, and collaboration with others in the organization.

Because the large majority of senior managers and directors are male, and because men are assumed to adhere more to masculine values than to feminine values, it seems that management cultures are still likely to be dominated by masculine norms and values.

Cultural preferences are also rooted in one's specific role in the organization; the culture preferences that are associated with specific role requirements may override gender differences.

There is strong empirical evidence that the managers' roles are more associated with masculine-typed than with feminine-typed values and characteristics.[6]

One study shows both female and male managers reported stronger preferences for masculine culture than did female and male employees at lower levels.

Masculine culture preferences are especially assumed to affect employees' motives to advance in their careers. . . . When starting their careers, women feel less attracted to masculine cultures than men do; however, once they have reached a management position in the organization, their preference is similar to those of men. This would imply that only those women who have the capacity to adapt their preferences to the masculine dominant cultural values are selected for leadership.[7]

It's clear that providing a clear-cut ideal for a corporate culture is not simple, but it's not impossible, either.

The Characteristics of a Corporate Culture that Advances Women

One of the best ways for leaders to establish a corporate culture that advances women is to first decide that it is important to do so, and then to develop a corporate blueprint for the new culture. Consider the following characteristics and how they can advance women in your culture:

1. Positive assumptions in executive ranks about women, their abilities, and their commitment to careers;

2. Perceptions that women fit in the corporate culture;

3. Career planning and the range of job experience commensurate with the future needs of the organization;

4. Core opportunities for female employees for potential management;

5. Women relocating for career advancement;

6. Managers accountable for advancing women;

7. Management giving women line experience;

8. Succession planning is established;

9. Positive mentoring and self-selection helping women move into leadership positions;

10. Mentoring and inclusion in informal career networks;

11. Uniform appraisal and compensation systems for men and women;

12. Corporate systems designed for large-scale infusion for women such as flexible work arrangements;

13. Forms of "cultural encouragement" and support for work-family initiatives and commitment to diversity programs; and

14. A ban on female discrimination and sexual harassment.[8]

By purposefully considering these characteristics, leaders can incorporate many of them into a women's initiative to develop a culture that advances women and benefits the entire organization.

Creating Purposeful Cultural Change to Advance Women

When considering a women's initiative, it is essential to understand that cultural change is not easy and creating sustainable improvements is difficult. It takes top executive support to set the tone for change, and then it takes vision and direction to initiate and establish the improvements. It also takes great effort to keep the initiative fresh and relevant. The rewards are well worth it.

One company's leaders found that it took five to six years to see real improvements. They also found that the changes created a positive desired change in the culture. And, it required effort to keep the women's initiative relevant given changes in the economy, the industry, and even in their own company.[9]

It is also important to understand that societal changes have to be considered in light of a women's initiative. Consider the following.

A new term describes high-income female providers: alpha earners. A demographic study found that 11 percent of marriages feature an alpha earner wife.[10] In 2001, more than 30.7 percent of married households with a working wife, the wife's income exceeded the husband's earnings.[11]

The average woman's wage still trails a man's, 76 cents to the dollar. The level of income a woman brings into the household generally correlates with her participation in family financial and career decisions.[12]

Giving attention to these types of changes will certainly keep a women's initiative current and positive results will follow.

How a Women's Initiative Can Influence Organizational Culture

Without a doubt, an organization's culture is influenced when an effective women's initiative is in place. When the CEO and other leaders get behind the initiative by making the development of women a core value and make it a high priority, it can have significant positive influence on the culture and on the bottom line

> *It takes top executive support to set the tone for change and then it takes vision and direction to initiate and establish the improvements.*

One company recognizes that the presence of a women's initiative is a competitive advantage:

> *The initiative has helped us retain very high talented women, but has also developed them for future opportunities.*

As one leader described his vision for the company:

> *I just want to try to think about how to make this a place where everyone would want his wife or daughter or sister to work.*

One company has gone so far as to include a complete organization for its women's initiative with an executive national director that reports to the CEO. This demonstrates the commitment of the CEO to the very existence of the initiative. The company has experienced many successes of their women's initiative.

As one leader shared:

The initiative is seen as something that not only affects women, but men as well. A lot of the changes that were made over the years have really made our culture better for everyone.

A sustainable women's initiative is integrated with other management processes. Policies and procedures state the expectation that jobs and the women's initiative are important to the company and their people. Policies and procedures are proactively recognized and address the women's initiative.

During interviews in one company, leaders noted that the women's initiative was an integral part of succession planning and the performance review process. Additionally, in every interview, the leaders mentioned that the women's initiative had played a key role in their own development as leaders within the company.

As one leader put it:

I think it's given me a tremendous opportunity and has really advanced my career substantially.

Another leader mentioned:

This initiative has impacted me personally. I'm a mom and that affects everything about my life and my work. I work from home 100 percent of the time. I live in a city and work in a place where we don't even have a company office.

It is apparent that when the company's executive leadership team values the women's initiative, this directly influences the attitudes throughout the company. The expectation that the initiative is a core value and a high priority motivates employees at all levels of the company to strive for a high amount of inclusion throughout the organization.

The leaders in one company indicate that the women's initiative includes both women and men and many of the best practices within the initiative have helped the entire organization.

One leader stated:

Women will disproportionably benefit from the changes made by the women's initiative in the early years, but at the end of the day, they really benefit all of us, and a major intent of our women's initiative is that the activities of the initiative benefit the firm as a whole.

The leaders were also very proud of the fact that they were the first company to pursue a women's initiative and felt that much of the initiative's success was due to the CEO's positive stance on building a very strong organization that included women. A number of leaders described how they have been involved in the women's initiative and how it has affected the culture and the organization.

Leaders commented:

The initiative really was about creating an environment that was inclusive for everyone. I'm going to go to this women's initiative event on Wednesday; it's not a big deal. People are just so used to having a women's initiative around, and it becomes part of the way that we do business. It is a defining part of who we are, which, I think, is really positive. Employees are encouraged to openly discuss the women's initiative and they feel comfortable doing so because of the support from management at all levels in the organization.

Another leader stated:

The company executives realize it's important and that it ensures the culture is being impacted by the women's initiative. The company realizes that we can't grow our business without women, and they realize that everything we do seems to affect our entire culture, and the CEO is in support of it.

Some leaders also expressed their confidence that the program would help their company be an even better place to work in the future.

This company is a place that really does treat women well and works to advance them. The women's initiative accrues benefits for the entire firm. The women's initiative is somewhere between a nine and a ten on a scale of one to ten with a ten as high.

An organization may characterize itself as women-friendly—or not. However, if your organization wants to be successful in the twenty-first century with its global competition, a women's initiative may provide the structure required to support such a culture.

∽

Things to Consider

❑ How would an outsider describe our corporate culture?

❑ How does our corporation favor female gender, positively?

❑ What evidence supports or rejects that the glass ceiling effect is evident in our company?

❑ When was the last time our company made a major organizational change?

❑ How does our culture produce any difference in the ratio of females and males in the top levels of our company's leadership?

*D*eveloping leadership
and facilitating growth in
individuals through mentoring
is a key deliverable
of a women's initiative.

Chapter 6

Maximizing Through Mentoring

My research shows that mentoring is the number one influence in helping women in the workplace achieve their full potential.

What is Mentoring?

The origins of the word mentor come from Greek mythology. In Homer's *The Odyssey*, the goddess Athena took the shape of the nobleman Mentor. Mentor was a counselor/teacher asked by Odysseus to watch over his son Telemachus during Odysseus' long voyage. Mentor guided and nurtured the boy until Odysseus returned many years later.[1]

The ability to communicate enables humans to learn from each other. Each generation passes on the knowledge to the following one. Without formally putting the name mentoring on the process, humans naturally mentor each other. Mentoring means to facilitate, guide, and encourage continuous innovation, learning, and growth to prepare for the future. Mentoring is about being real, being a catalyst, and sometimes being a kind of prophet. It is, therefore, far more art than science.[2]

Mentoring, one form of learning, is acquired in individually meaningful ways.[3] Adults are motivated to learn as they develop needs and interests that learning will satisfy. Consider the following five concepts about mentoring and learning:

1. Mentee's needs and interests are the appropriate starting points for any mentoring relationship.

2. Adult learning is typically life or work centered. The appropriate frameworks for organizing mentoring are life and/or work-related situations, not academic or theoretical subjects.

3. Experience is the richest resource for adult learning. The approach for mentoring involves active participation in a planned series of experiences, the analysis of those experiences, and their application to work and life situations.

4. Adults have a deep need to be self-directing. The role of the mentor is to engage in a process of inquiry, analysis, and decision making with the mentee, rather than to transmit knowledge and then evaluate the mentee's conformity to it.

5. Individual differences among adults increase with age and experience. Mentoring must make optimum provision for differences in style, time, place, and pace of learning.

Types of Mentoring

Mentoring can be approached from various aspects: hierarchical, peer, team, and gender. It can also be formal or informal in nature. Mentoring in business is most effective when targeted at four levels: the individual worker, the management team, other working groups, and the entire organization and its culture.

Historically, mentoring has been more of a hierarchical relationship with the mentor being at a more senior level in the organization than the mentee. With flatter organizational structures, mentoring is now often approached peer-to-peer and often comes from networking relationships both internal and external to the organization. This type of mentoring relationship can develop strong working relationships and build self-confidence of peers.[4]

My research shows that mentoring is the number one influence in helping women in the workplace achieve their full potential.

Team mentoring is an emerging approach. Some organizations have recognized that one-to-one mentoring relationships can be problematic in terms of time availability and narrow scope. To overcome these barriers, a team of mentors can be assigned to a mentee in a many-to-one relationship.[5] Many organizations recognize the important benefits of mentoring and have attempted to create formal mentoring programs. This is a significant development for women, who face greater barriers in finding informal mentoring relationships than men, due to both the lack of female role models at the top and the knowledge that this is important for leadership development.

Formal mentoring programs within corporations and professions give high potential women access to upper level managers and executives who can aid and advance their careers. Most often a selection process exists in which managers nominate a candidate who is then assigned a mentor based on criteria important to the mentee. Next follows training sessions for the participants in how to be mentees and mentors. The mentees meet with their mentors to identify goals, develop a contract, and schedule time to meet. The program usually has two objectives—the development of individuals and the development of diversity within the company. On an individual level, a mentee often wants to expand her experience and extend her willingness to take risks.

In my twenty-eight years of working in Corporate America, I have had both formal and informal mentoring relationships within the business world. I have found both are effective. The effectiveness of the mentoring program is based on the relationship you develop with the mentor or mentee. It is all about sharing experiences and creating a level of trust with this person. Both the mentor and mentee gain from this relationship.

Why Mentoring is So Important for Women

Mentors are an important factor in the career success of women and men, but even more so for women. Gender issues have become increasingly significant as the role of mentoring in career development has been recognized. More males are mentors than females due to organizational demographics.[6] In addition, the higher a woman rises, the more difficult it is to find a mentor, female or male, and many potential mentors are competitors. Young women in organizations benefit from female mentors who are experienced in the integration of career and family.

A Gallup poll of 561 full-time executive and professional women revealed that women under age thirty-five are more likely to have mentors than their older counterparts (60 percent of younger women had mentors and 48 percent of older women had mentors). Fifty-six percent of these mentors were women. Studies confirm women with mentors report greater career success and higher job satisfaction than women without a mentor.[7]

With so few women in high-level positions, females have few opportunities to learn from the experiences of role models. Watching experienced women handle challenging business situations has opened a new range of strategies they can transfer to their own daily work experiences.

While this opportunity is relatively new to women, it has been the norm for men for many years.

Mentoring can support two aspects of a woman's work life: psychosocial and career development.[8] The psychosocial function enriches the mentee's sense of competence and effectiveness and includes role modeling, acceptance and confirmation, counseling, and friendship. The career development functions include sponsorship, exposure and visibility, coaching, and preparations for advancement through challenging assignments. When a hierarchical relationship provides all of these functions, it best approximates the prototype of a mentor relationship. A woman can benefit from a mentoring relationship by gaining greater career identity and improved self-confidence.

Mentoring can help women form and maintain working relationships. The maintenance of relationships in the workplace is more important to women than to men and is the most significant difference between the genders. Women who have a successful relationship with a peer, executive, and/or mentor create a friendship that builds on each other's personalities, and also creates synergy with that female as a role model and a friend. In corporate cultures, it is important to have both female and male role models as one moves into executive roles.

Women often have different needs and concerns from their male counterparts, which can be addressed in successful mentoring relationships. Women typically face a complex, interrelated set of career issues that may be outside men's experiences. These differences may make it difficult for senior men to understand and provide the support required for women to advance in their careers.

Women bring unique competencies and requirements to the mentor relationship. The emotional aspects of the relationship are more vital for female mentees than for male mentees and women are more likely than men to stress caring, nurturing, and teaching when describing the mentoring relationship.[9] Relationships involving a female mentee are also more likely to develop into a close friendship than are those involving only men.

Whether in ancient Greece or modern corporations, mentoring is a valuable tool for training and developing leaders, particularly for women in business. One of the challenges for a woman is to decide to find a mentor to help her become a better leader. She must first accept that she can learn to lead and then determine to improve herself through a mentoring relationship and other alliances. Success comes when both the mentee and the mentor understand that a mentoring relationship requires a commitment along with opportunities to exercise and apply leadership skills.

All the elements of a dynamic leader may exist in an individual, but those elements may never be revealed or utilized if the opportunity to lead does not occur. If too many leaders already are at the top of an organization, if the organization does not recognize leader potential in a particular individual, or if situations never occur that allow the leader to step forward and move ahead, leadership qualities will never become evident. Mentoring relationships can provide opportunities for women to practice and demonstrate leadership.

How a Women's Initiative Can Foster Mentoring

All of the leaders interviewed believed mentoring was important to the initiative. All of the leaders mentioned they had a mentor, and over the years many of them have had more than one.

One leader who had been a women's initiative regional leader for several years asked a younger woman to help chair the women's initiative in her region. She found this a beneficial experience because it gave the younger woman a chance to learn and it provided a way to build leadership. This act of assimilation of a newer woman into the process fosters leadership in the individual and at the group level for the company.

Developing leadership and facilitating growth in individuals through mentoring is a key deliverable of a women's initiative.

In creating the women's initiative at one company, I found mentoring enabled women to have role models and learn how to be successful in their current and future positions. I reached out to one hundred executives, received buy-in from them, and then opened up the mentoring program to women who wanted to be mentees. The six-month program was a success, and, in almost all cases, a bond was created between mentor and mentee that went beyond the program's time limit.

By the way, before we go to the next subject, let me encourage any women reading this book to reach out to a colleague, peer, or executive to ask for a mentoring relationship. Learning the value of taking risks may help; when you ask for that next promotion, go for it!

~

Things to Consider

❑ How does our company provide for mentoring of employees?

❑ What training does our company provide for mentors?

❑ How do our leaders provide mentoring opportunities for both female and male employees?

❑ How are mentors accountable for reporting on the progress of the one being mentored?

❑ What examples of individuals gaining promotion due to effective mentoring can be cited within the company?

Having a women's initiative changes not only the people and culture, but ultimately improves decision making and the bottom line of the company.

Chapter 7

Answering the Burning Question

The burning question is this: Does a women's initiative foster executive leadership in women?

The answer is a resounding YES!

Overall, a company's experience with its women's initiative has obviously changed its culture. First, the organization has shifted from including only males in executive positions to now including both females and males at the senior levels. The numbers of females in leadership positions has increased three-fold. The company is now an employer of choice among college graduates and experienced business leaders. Ultimately, this company will have a tremendous advantage in choosing the most qualified candidates from both gender pools.

> *The burning question is this: does a women's initiative foster executive leadership in women? The answer is YES!*

Other companies have recently cited significant success as a result of their women's initiative: Goldman Sachs, PepsiCo, PricewaterhouseCoopers, and Scotiabank.[1]

Goldman Sachs' Senior Women's initiative supports women in their career growth, engagement, advancement, and retention. The initiative provides networking opportunities for senior-level women and strives to remove barriers to advancement. From 2001 to 2006, the number of women in senior-level positions has doubled in the company.

PepsiCo's Women of Color Multicultural Alliance's focus on attracting, retaining, and developing women of color has similarly resulted in more women in senior positions. A major feature of the initiative is to develop more authentic relationships across all levels in the organization.

PricewaterhouseCoopers' (PwC) initiative focuses on building a culture where differences are valued. The Unique People Experience has increased productivity and reduced turnover. A major element of the initiative is to move from a traditional means of getting work done to a more team-focused approach. As a result, women's participation rate at the partner level and above has risen more than 30 percent in the last five years.

Scotiabank has nearly doubled the number of women at the vice president level and above in the last three years as a result of its Advancement of Women initiative.

It is important for a company to be diverse in its thinking, leadership, and employees. Having a women's initiative changes not only the people and culture, but ultimately improves decision making and the bottom line of the company. Be the company with the advantage.

∼

Things to Consider

- ❑ Which of the results realized by the companies listed in this chapter benefit our company?

- ❑ How valuable is the women's initiative as a tool for our company?

- ❑ Who, along with me, can take the lead in introducing the concept of the women's initiative to our company leaders?

A women's initiative creates
a tremendous advantage
around recruitment and choosing
the most qualified candidates
from both gender pools.

References

Chapter 1

[1] Evans, G. (2000). *Play Like a Man, Win Like a Woman*. New York: Broadway Books.

[2] Catalyst. (2000). *2000 Catalyst Census of Women Corporate Top Officers and Top Earners*. New York: Catalyst.

[3] Catalyst. (2000). *2000 Catalyst Census of Women Corporate Top Officers and Top Earners*. New York: Catalyst.

[4] Evans, G. (2000). *Play Like a Man, Win Like a Woman*. New York: Broadway Books.

[5] *Global Employment Trends for Women 2004*. (2004). International Labour Office. Retrieved from www.ilo.org/public/english/employment/strat/stratprod.htm. Accessed February 4, 2005.

[6] Blau, F. D., Ferber, M. A., & Winkler, A. E. (1998). *The Economics of Women, Men, and Work*. Upper Saddle River, N.J.: Prentice Hall.

[7] *Global Employment Trends for Women 2004*. (2004). International Labour Office. Retrieved from www.ilo.org/public/english/employment/strat/stratprod.htm. Accessed February 7, 2005.

[8] Nadler, D. A., & Tushman, M. L. (1999) "Beyond the Charismatic Leader: Leadership and Organizational Change" *California Management Review*, 77-96.

[9] Kouzes, J. M., & Posner, B. Z. (1993). *Credibility.* San Francisco: Jossey-Bass: 323.

[10] Burke, R. J., & Nelson, D. L. (2002). *Advancing Women's Dareers.* Oxford, UK: Blackwell Publishing: 6.

[11] Catalyst. (2000). *2000 Catalyst Census of Women Corporate Top Officers and Top Earners.* New York: Catalyst.

[12] Catalyst. (2004). *The Bottom Line: Connecting Corporate Performance and Gender Diversity.* Retrieved from http://www.catalystwomen.org. Accessed February 4, 2005.

Chapter 2

[1] Catalyst. (2004). *The Bottom Line: Connecting Corporate Performance and Gender Diversity.* Retrieved from http://www.catalystwomen.org. Accessed February 4, 2005.

Chapter 3

[1] Greenleaf, R. K. (1977). *Servant Leadership: A Journey into the Nature of Legitimate Power and Greatness.* Mahwah, NJ: Paulist Press.

[2] Goleman, D. (1998). *Working with Emotional Intelligence.* New York: Bantam.p. pxii).

[3] Mayer, J. D., & Salovey, P. (1995). "Emotional Intelligence and the Construction and Regulation of Feelings." *Applied & Preventive Psychology,* 4(3), 197-208.

[4] Bass, B. M. (1990). *Bass and Stogdill's Handbook of Leadership.* New York: The Free Press.

[5] Shamir, B., Zakay, E., Breinin, E., & Popper, M. (1998). "Correlates of Charismatic Leader Behavior in Military Units: Subordinates' Attitudes, Unit Characteristics, and Superiors' Appraisals of Leader Performance." *Academy of Management Journal,* 41, 387-409.

[6] Lowe, K. B., Kroeck, K. G., & Sivasubramaniam, N. (1996). "Effectiveness Correlates of Transformational and Transactional Leadership: A Meta-analytic Review." *Leadership Quarterly*, 7, 385-425

Chapter 4

[1] Wachs, E. (2000). *Why the Best Man for the Job is a Woman*. New York: HarperInformation, p. 56.

[2] Eccles, J. S. (1985). *The Gifted and Talented: Developmental Perspectives. Why Doesn't Jane Run? Sex Differences in Educational and Occupational Patterns*. Washington: American Psychological Association.

[3] Hewlett, S. (April, 2002). "Executive Women and the Myth of Having it All." *Harvard Business Review*, 66-73.

[4] Orenstein, P. (2000). *Flux Women on Sex, Work, Love, Kids and Life in a Half-changed World*. New York: Doubleday.

[5] Swiss, D. J. (1996). *Women Breaking Through*. Princeton, N.J.: Pacesetter Books. p. 142.

[6] Wong, T. Ohls (2005) "Fostering Executive Leadership in Women." A published dissertation. Capella University, Minneapolis, MN.

Chapter 5

[1] Schein, E. H. (1996). "Three Cultures of Management: The Key to Organizational Learning." *MIT Sloan Management Review*, 38(1), 9 - 20.

[2] Swiss, D. J. (1996). *Women Breaking Through*. Princeton, N.J.: Pacesetter Books: 206.

[3] Hojgaard, L. (2002). "Tracing Differentiation in Gendered Leadership: An Analysis of Differences in Gender Composition in Top Management in Business, Politics, and the Civil Service." *Gender, Work and Organization*, 9(1), 15-38.

[4] Van Vianen, A. E. M. (2002). ""Illuminating the Glass Ceiling: The Role of Organizational Culture Preferences." *Journal of Occupational and Organization Psychology*, 75(3), 315-338.

[5] Maier, M. (1999). "On the Gendered Substructure of Organization: Dimensions and Dilemmas of Corporate Masculinity." In G. N. Powell (Ed.), *Handbook of Gender and Work* (pp. 69-94) Thousand Oaks, CA: Sage.

[6] Powell, G. N. (1993). *Women and Men in Management.* Newbury Park, CA.: Sage, 174.

[7] Van Vianen, A. E. M. (2002). "Illuminating the Glass Ceiling: The Role of Organizational Culture Preferences." *Journal of Occupational and Organization Psychology*, 75(3), 315-338.

[8] Landmark Study, HR Focus (1998) p. 6

[9] Wong, T. Ohls (2005) "Fostering Executive Leadership in Women." A published dissertation. Capella University, Minneapolis, MN.

[10] Bianchi, S. (2001). "Alpha Earners." *Times Online*, May. Abstract retrieved from http://www. timesonline.co.uk/article. Accessed February 7, 2005.

[11] Weiss, J. (May 12, 2003). "She Works, He Doesn't." *Newsweek*, 44-52.

[12] Setlow, C. (September 21, 1998). "Dual Income Doesn't Mean Dual Decision-making." *Discount Store News*, 37(18), 19.

Chapter 6

[1] Fritts, P. J. (1998). *The New Managerial Mentor.* Palo Alto, CA: Davis-Black.

[2] Bell, C. R. (1996). *Managers as Mentors.* San Francisco: Berrett-Koehler.

[3] Knowles, M. (1990). *The Adult Learner: A Neglected Species.* Houston: Gulg.

[4] Kram, K. E., & Isabella, L. A. (1985). "Mentoring Alternatives: T he Role of Peer Relationships in Career Development." *Academy of Management Journal,* 28(1), 110-132.

[5] Kram, K. (1988). *Mentoring at Work: Development Relationships in Organizational Life.* Lanham, MD.: University Press of America.

[6] Morrison, A. M., White, R. P., & Van Velsor, E. (1987). *Breaking the Glass Ceiling.* Reading, MA: Addison Wesley.

[7] Duff, C. (1999). *Learning from Other Women.* New York: American Management Association: 8.

[8] Kram, K. (1988). *Mentoring at Work: Development Relationships in Organizational Life.* Lanham, MD.: University Press of America.

[9] Reich, M. A. (1985). "Executive Views from Both Sides of Mentoring." *Personnel,* 62, 42-46.

Chapter 7

[1] Business Leaders and Experts Discuss Issues Facing Women in the Workplace at 2007 Catalyst Awards Conference: 2007 Catalyst Awards Conference features Catalyst Award-winning initiatives from Goldman Sachs, PepsiCo, PricewaterhouseCoopers, and Scotiabank, March 21, 2007. www.catalystwomen.org. Accessed March 23, 2007.

About the Author

 Dr. Tammy Wong's professional career spans over three decades of sales, marketing, and strategy experience in Fortune 500 companies. She is known for her demonstrated leadership abilities and her commitment to develop leadership in others.

She is the CEO and Founder of Fostering Executive Leadership, Inc. She works with companies that want to make a difference in their organizations by developing, advancing, and retaining women and ultimately becoming an employer of choice.

Before starting her own company, Dr. Wong worked in the technology industry for companies such as IBM, Xerox, and Sun Microsystems advancing into many leadership roles. At Sun, she founded and was the president of the women's organization that included over two thousand women worldwide. With this achievement, she was recognized by her peers when they selected her for the highly coveted "Making a Difference" award.

Dr. Wong's extensive education includes a B.S. in Economics from St. Mary's College and an M.B.A. from Pepperdine University. She earned her Ph.D. in Business Organization and Management with an emphasis in Leadership. Her doctoral dissertation is titled "Fostering Executive Leadership in Women."

Tammy has served on the boards of several not-for-profit organizations and is a member of a select group of executive women who meet regularly to discuss leadership and business issues. She resides in Irvine, California, with her husband and five children and is active in her community.

Booking Information:
800-717-6250

Ordering Information

To order additional copies of this book, contact Dr. Tammy Wong at:

Office: 949.651.6250

Fax: 949.271.5665

Toll-free: 800.717.6250

You may email Tammy at:

Tammy@FosteringExecutiveLeadership.com

For more information, go to:

www.FosteringExecutiveLeadership.com